LEARNING THE ROPES

LEARNING THE ROPES

AN APPRENTICE IN THE LAST OF THE WINDJAMMERS

ERIC NEWBY

JOHN MURRAY

ACKNOWLEDGEMENTS

My thanks go to Hazel Wood, Caroline Knox and Barbara Smith of John Murray for their imaginative help with this book.

By the same author

A Short Walk in the Hindu Kush

Something Wholesale

Slowly Down the Ganges

The Last Grain Race

Love and War in the Appenines

The Big Red Train Ride

A Traveller's Life

A Book of Traveller's Tales

On the Shores of the Mediterranean

Round Ireland in Low Gear

A Small Place in Italy

World Atlas of Exploration

Great Ascents

A Merry Dance Around the World

What the Traveller Saw

© Eric Newby 1999

First published in 1999
by John Murray (Publishers) Ltd,
50 Albemarle Street, London W1X 4BD

Paperback edition 2000

The moral right of the author has been asserted.

A catalogue record for this book is available from the British Library

ISBN 0–7195–5641 4

Origination by Colourscript, Mildenhall, Suffolk

Printed and bound in Great Britain by Butler & Tanner Limited, Frome and London

TO THE MEN AND BOYS WHO SAILED IN *MOSHULU*

AND IN ALL THE OTHER SHIPS DURING THE LAST YEARS OF SQUARE SAIL

BEFORE THE SECOND WORLD WAR

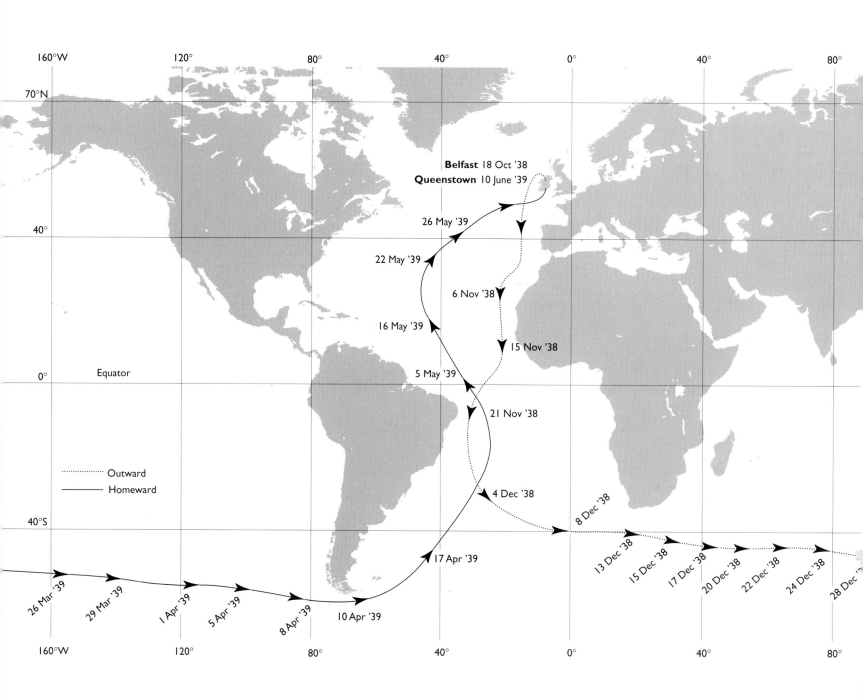

160°W   120°   80°   40°   0°   40°   80°

70°N

40°

Belfast 18 Oct '38
Queenstown 10 June '39

26 May '39

22 May '39

26 May '39

6 Nov '38

16 May '39

15 Nov '38

0°   Equator

5 May '39

21 Nov '38

Outward
Homeward

4 Dec '38   8 Dec '38

40°S

17 Apr '39   13 Dec '38   15 Dec '38   17 Dec '38   20 Dec '38   22 Dec '38   24 Dec '38   28 Dec '38

26 Mar '39   29 Mar '39   1 Apr '39   5 Apr '39   8 Apr '39   10 Apr '39

160°W   120°   80°   40°   0°   40°   80°

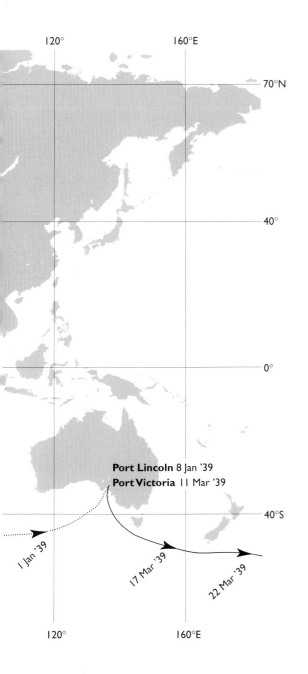

120°   160°E

70°N

40°

0°

Port Lincoln 8 Jan '39
Port Victoria 11 Mar '39

40°S

1 Jan '39

17 Mar '39

22 Mar '39

120°   160°E

CONTENTS

Acknowledgements   *4*

Map of Moshulu's *course round the world*   *6*

INTRODUCTION   *9*

PHOTOGRAPHS   *36*

AFTERWARDS   *142*

The Grain Race 1939: *ships and passage times*   *144*

MOSHULU, ex *DREADNOUGH*T, ex *KURT*

Four-masted steel barque

5,300 tons d.w., 3,116 gross, 2,911 net.

Built by William Hamilton, Port Glasgow, 1904

It was the summer of 1938 when I wrote to the Finnish shipowner Gustav Erikson asking for a job. I was eighteen, and my recent brief career in advertising had suggested that I was not really cut out for office life. But I had always been attracted by the sea, and on my way back from a seaside holiday in Devon that summer I impulsively wrote to Mr Erikson offering myself as an apprentice on one of his sailing ships. I received an almost immediate reply telling me to get in touch with the firm's London agents, Messrs H. Clarkson of Bishopsgate, and in October 1938, with the Munich crisis coming to the boil, I crossed on the night boat from Heysham to join the Erikson Line ship *Moshulu*, a four-masted square-rigged barque, in Belfast.

I had learned about Erikson from my friend Mr Mountstewart, an eccentric personality with a passion for sail. Throughout my time at the advertising agency Mr Mountstewart had been sowing the seeds of discontent, urging me to give it up and go to sea because 'time was running out'. By this he did not mean that soon there would be a war, but that soon there would be no more great sailing ships plying the seas for me to sail on. How right he was. Though I did not know it at the time, the voyage I was about to make in *Moshulu* would be the last of the annual voyages the great square riggers would make carrying grain back to Europe from the South Australian wheat belt. Within a short time there would be no more steel square-rigged sailing ships left trading on the oceans of the world. In 1938 there were still a dozen or so, vying with one another each spring to make the shortest passage home, but the Second World War would bring their trading days to an end.

Gustav Erikson of Mariehamn in the Baltic was the last man to own a great fleet of sailing ships. By the late 1930s the grain trade with South Australia was the only one left in which ships like his could engage with any real hope of making a profit, and then only if the owner had an obsessional interest in reducing his running costs, which Erikson had – hence, probably, his prompt reply. He had to pay his crew – which had to be as small as possible commensurate with safety – as little as possible. He could not afford to insure his ships, most of which he had bought at shipbreakers' prices; but he had to maintain them to such a standard of excellence that they were all given top rating by Lloyd's and the other Register Societies. He had to be respected and feared by the ships' masters he employed as a hard man over whose eyes no one could pull any wool, for if they were frightened of him then the tremors would be felt even by the newest apprentice in the fleet.

Gustav Erikson employed no public relations men to improve his image. I never met any foremast hand who liked him – it would be as reasonable to expect any British citizen today to 'like' the Inspector of Taxes – and in our ship he was known as 'Ploddy Gustav', although most of us had never set eyes on him. The thing that warmed one to him was the certainty that he was completely indifferent to whether anyone liked him or not. He was only interested in his crews in so far as they were necessary to sail his ships efficiently, and for that reason he made sure that they were adequately and decently fed by sailing ship standards, and that the ships they manned were supplied with enough rope, canvas, paint and other necessary gear to enable them to be thoroughly seaworthy at all times. It is difficult to see what more he could have done.

He certainly knew about ships. In fact he knew as much about his own ships as the men who sailed them. He had gone to sea as a boy of nine, got his first command, in a North Sea sailing vessel, at the age of nineteen, and had been master of a number of square-rigged vessels before becoming an owner.

The South Australian grain trade was peculiarly suited to sailing ships such as

Erikson's. Spencer Gulf, to which the ships came to load their cargoes, is a 180-mile-long inlet in the south coast of Australia, off the Great Australian Bight. The water in Spencer Gulf is shallow but a sailing vessel can navigate almost the entire length of it. It lies in the very heart of the wheat belt, and behind the little ports on either side wheat fields stretch away to the horizon. With one or two exceptions these ports are, or were, very primitive. Some had jetties where the ships could lie alongside (the one at Port Germein was over a mile long), but at others they had to lie offshore and load the bags of grain into their holds from lightering ketches. What kept the majority of steamers away from the Gulf was the fact that there was no import trade at these ports. This meant that any ship coming in to load had to make the outward voyage to Australia loaded with ballast, and this was not a paying proposition for the majority of steamships.

Although the waters of the Great Australian Bight are dangerous and inhospitable for ships of any kind, the Gulf itself was in some ways extraordinarily convenient for sailing ships. It lies only 5 degrees north of the most powerful wind-belt in the world, the Roaring Forties, and almost exactly at the half-way point for a sailing vessel on a round-the-world passage from Europe by way of the Cape of Good Hope and Cape Horn. There could be maddening delays both on entering and leaving the Gulf due to calms, but once out in the Bight on the homeward voyage, it was often not more than a day or so before the ship picked up the westerlies for the run to the Horn, over 6,000 sea miles.

The normal practice for ships like *Moshulu* which were engaged in this trade was to sail from Europe about the last week of September or the first week of October in ballast, use the north and south-east trade winds in the North and South Atlantic Oceans, and run before the westerlies across the Southern Indian Ocean,

Moshulu's Captain, Mikael Sjögren, in 1938.

making what might well be the first landfall of the entire voyage at the lighthouse on the South Neptune Islands at the entrance to Spencer Gulf. Then, unless the loading port was already known, a ship would generally sail to Port Lincoln, near the mouth of the Gulf, and lie offshore until a freight was fixed and orders were received to proceed to the loading port. Thus ended a journey of some 15,000 sea miles. A good outward passage for a ship in ballast was around eighty days, although passages of a hundred days and more were common.

It might be weeks or even months before a freight was fixed. As soon as it was, the ship would sail to the loading port; but first the crew had to get rid of the ballast, shovelling it into baskets, hoisting it out of the hold with the temperature often up in the hundreds and tipping it over the side at the offshore ballast grounds. Few sailing ships had water ballast tanks. It was not possible to jettison all the ballast at once, and one or more trips under sail had to be made to the ballast grounds in the intervals of loading the cargo.

This was itself frequently interrupted by the strong breezes which spring up quickly in the Gulf and blow for a day or so at a time. Loading was a long enough business without these delays. The bags of grain had first to be put into the lightering ketches and brought out to the ship and loaded. A 3,000-ton barque like the *Moshulu* could take more than 60,000 sacks of grain, about 5,000 tons. With such arrangements a twelve-week turnaround between arrival in the Gulf and departure for Europe was not uncommon.

The normal date of departure for Europe from Spencer Gulf varied between the last week in February and the last week in March, although a ship which had been lucky enough to secure a cargo of timber from Finland to East Africa on the outward voyage or a charter to load guano at one of the lonely islands in the Indian

Ocean for New Zealand, might arrive at the Gulf later and leave later. Sailing for Europe in February or March and making a really good passage of a hundred days for the 15,000-mile voyage by way of the Horn, the ships usually reached Falmouth or Queenstown (now Cobh) in the Irish Republic some time between the first fortnight in June and the middle of July. It could take half as long again but the charterer was not worried: providing it was kept dry, grain was not a perishable cargo and whoever happened to own it at any particular time – for it often changed hands several times during the voyage – was getting free warehousing for his cargo while it was at sea.

Some of the smaller and more ancient ships and cargo-carrying cadet ships would return to Europe sailing westwards by way of the Cape of Good Hope, but although the route was about 1,200 miles shorter it was much slower and they rarely made the passages which the Cape Horners were capable of. (The best ever recorded Cape Horn passage – sixty-six days – was made by the British steel barque *Swanhilda* in 1899, a remarkable performance that came within a few days of equalling that of the wool clippers which began their voyage on the east coast of Australia, up to a thousand miles and several days' sailing to the east of Spencer Gulf.)

Nearly all the Erikson ships discharged their cargoes in the United Kingdom and when they had done so they would either go into dry dock at the port of discharge, or go back to Mariehamn, their home port, in the Åland Islands in the Baltic, and dry dock at Copenhagen in preparation for the autumn. By the time they reached home their hulls would be very foul, having been afloat for nine or ten months and having sailed some 30,000 sea miles.

Some of the best and most powerful ships that Erikson possessed were originally German-owned and built for the Chilean nitrate trade. *Moshulu* was one of these.

'Op the rigging.'

14   The sailing ship trade in nitrate, which was used extensively before 1914 as a fertilizer, barely survived the first war. It persisted into the 1920s but this was virtually the end of it, apart from two German barques, *Padua* and *Priwall*, which loaded nitrate into the late '30s. Until 1914 Chile had supplied 90 per cent of the world's nitrate needs; but the First World War brought about such an increase in the production of artificial nitrates that by 1935 Chile was supplying only 15 per cent of the world's consumption. Germany, whose fleet of sailing ships was one of the two greatest carriers of nitrate in the world, was foremost in the development of synthetic nitrates, the production of which, together with the opening of the Panama Canal, enabled liners to devote part of their carrying space to nitrate, ending the sailing ship's participation in the trade for all practical purposes.

For sailing ships the nitrate trade was one of the toughest in the world. The voyage from the Channel outward round the Horn in the teeth of the prevailing westerly winds was hard and dangerous. The nitrate ports themselves on the western seaboard of Chile, on what was known as 'The Flaming Coast' – Tocopilla, Pisagua, Caleta Buena, Mejillones, Iquique, Antofagasta and Taltal, to name some of the principal ones – were mostly inhospitable places, lacking amenities. Some were nothing more than shanty towns and collections of adobe huts with a population that was a hotch-potch of native stevedores (whose job it was to load the ships with the nitrate from lighters), agents, sailors who had deserted their ships, owners of halls in which the fandango was danced nightly, and pimps and prostitutes; places which were remembered, nevertheless, by old sailors with great nostalgia.

The anchorages were often dangerously exposed, either to the exceptionally violent winds known as 'northers', which sprang up with little warning, or to tidal waves which were the aftermath to the sometimes violent *terremotos*, the earthquakes which frequently convulsed the littoral. Unless a vessel could find shelter from them it would either founder or else be thrown several hundred yards up on the shore where it would remain as a sort of monument.

Navigation on the coast was difficult. In opposition to the northerly winds was the coastal current which had a strong northerly set. It was so strong that if a ship made its landfall to the north of its destined port – no uncommon thing, especially for ships which had crossed the Pacific from Australia with a cargo of coal for a Chilean port – it might take a month to reach its destination against it. The coast itself was, and still is, horrible – hot, dusty, treeless, earthquake-prone and backed by desert and desiccated, waterless mountains. Behind it, in the unimaginable interior, were the nitrate mines.

By 1914 two great fleets of sailing ships, one French, the other German, more or less dominated the nitrate trade, that of Antonin Dominique Bordes et Fils of Bordeaux, and Ferdinand Laeisz's 'Flying P' line of Hamburg. Dom Bordes, a firm whose origins went back to the 1840s, really began to take a serious interest in the nitrate business in the 1880s, when it started buying and commissioning iron and steel barques and ships, most of which were built in Scottish yards. They were beautiful vessels which could be readily identified at sea by their graceful lines and black-and-white painted ports. By 1914 there were forty-six of them with a carrying capacity of over 160,000 tons; but by 1918 enemy action had accounted for twenty-two.

Up to that time the French merchant marine had had the advantage of a government subsidized navigation bounty which amounted to Fr.1.70 a gross ton for every thousand miles sailed or steamed, as well as a generous building bounty. Under this benign protection France's sailing ship tonnage increased while that of other nations declined, but the danger of the subsidies was that they provided owners with an unnatural protection and when they were withdrawn at the end of the war Dom Bordes was unprepared to compete without them and the fleet simply melted away.

Laeisz's 'Flying P' line – the names of all their ships began with the letter P – was, like Dom Bordes, largely built up in the 1880s and 1890s; but unlike the French, the Germans were not protected by subsidies. By 1914 Laeisz's nitrate fleet was the most efficiently run fleet of sailing ships in the world. In its heyday it included the two most powerful sailing ships ever built, the five-masted steel barque *Potosi* and the five-masted ship *Preussen*.

There was nothing freakish about either ship except their size and performance. Both had the capacity with winds of the right strength and in the right quarter to storm along at 16 knots, and with a favourable fresh gale, Force 8, both ships could and did average over 13 knots. Over the years in which they sailed for Laeisz, the consistently excellent passages they made read more like those of express trains than of sailing ships sailing out to Chile and home round the Horn twice a year. In some of their best performances, *Potosi* made the English Channel to the Chilean port of Valparaiso in fifty-five days, and from Iquique to the Channel in fifty-seven. *Preussen* made the Channel to Iquique in fifty-seven and Iquique to the Channel in sixty-eight.

But it was not by the performances of these two great ships that the achievement of the Laeisz fleet must be measured, but rather by the sheer consistency of the whole fleet. Ships like *Pommern*, *Pamir*, *Passat* and *Peking*, to name only a few, all made passages of under seventy days from the Channel to Valparaiso, and equally good ones home. Not all the Laeisz ships were German-built, but it was German captains who sailed them, and Laeisz who brought the loading arrangements at the nitrate ports to such a state of efficiency that the turnround of their ships was the fastest of all the ships engaged in the trade.

Laeisz lost their whole fleet to the Allies in 1918, though Ferdinand Laeisz succeeded in buying back a number of his ships from countries which had no idea of how to use them effectively. But the post-war shipping slump and the economic collapse of Germany forced him to disperse them again, and many of them went to Gustav Erikson and other Scandinavian owners. Nevertheless, Laeisz launched two more barques in the post-war years – *Priwall*, laid down in 1916 but not completed until 1920 because of the war, and *Padua*, launched in 1926. These were the last two commercial four-masted barques to be built, and the last of their kind.

Long before the war Laeisz had become convinced that, in spite of the remarkable performances of his two five-masted vessels, the most effective ship and the easiest to handle for the nitrate trade was a steel four-masted barque of around 3,000 tons, of three-island construction, steered from the raised bridge-deck amidships and fitted with brace and halliard winches. *Passat, Pamir* and *Peking* were all built to this specification and so were *Padua* and *Priwall*. Both these barques were worthy of their predecessors, but their most remarkable achievement occurred in 1936 in the grain trade, when both ships left the Elbe on the same tide and arrived together in Spencer Gulf sixty-six days later. *Padua* and *Priwall* and ships like them were the final flowering of centuries of maritime experience. Such a ship was the *Moshulu* of Mariehamn.

Moshulu was originally named *Kurt*. She was built, together with a sister ship, *Hans*, by William Hamilton of Port Glasgow for Siemers of Hamburg and they were both designed for the nitrate trade. The shipping firm of Siemers, one of the

Moshulu picking up the South-East Trades.

Pommern loading from a ketch in Spencer Gulf, South Australia.

oldest in Hamburg, had become involved in the nitrate trade at about the same time as Dom Bordes and Laeisz. It was not as large as the others, but by 1910 it owned six fine sailing ships as well as a number of steamships.

Kurt and *Hans* were the last two four-masted steel barques to be built by William Hamilton and were among the last to be built on the Clyde. They were built there because, at that time, they could not have been built as cheaply in a German yard to such a high standard of excellence. Completed, they each cost £36,000, and announcements of their launching appeared in Lloyd's Weekly Shipping Index. It would be interesting to speculate on how much they would cost today. They were both launched in the spring of 1904.

A month after *Kurt* was launched and rigged she left the Clyde for Port Talbot in South Wales. There she loaded coal and sailed for Chile on 21 June, arriving at Pisagua on 29 September, one hundred days out. Something must have delayed her because, according to Lloyd's Shipping Index, she did not sail from Iquique until 18 November 1904, from where she made a very slow passage of over a hundred days to the Channel, being off Beachy Head on 7 March 1905.

This was the first of seven outward voyages with coal from Welsh ports to the west coast of South America, nine voyages from Chile to Germany with nitrate, four ballast passages from South America's west coast ports to Newcastle, New South Wales, four passages from Australia to Chile loaded with coal and three passages from Hamburg to Santa Rosalia, Mexico, with coke and patent fuel for the copper smelting mines. The majority were not particularly outstanding, but what *Kurt* was really capable of was demonstrated in 1909 when, under her second captain Wilhelm Tönissen, she ran with a cargo of 4,920 tons of coal on board from Newcastle, New South Wales, to Valparaiso in 31 days 14 hours – 6,376 miles of sailing – a performance that has only been excelled on the same passage by two other vessels, the four-masted iron ship *Wendur* and the four-masted iron barque *Loch Torridon*.

In August 1914 both *Kurt* and her sister ship *Hans* were at Santa Rosalia, on the western shores of the Gulf of California in Mexico, a place as unattractive and desolate as any nitrate port but popular with sailors, to which they had gone with cargoes of coke and patent fuel for the copper smelting plant. *Hans* was on her eleventh voyage, *Kurt* on her tenth. There *Hans* lay with eleven other German sailing ships, at first sheltering from the war and later interned from 1914 to 1920, when they were all bought by the Robert Dollar Company of San Francisco through the Reparations Committee in Washington.

Hans was renamed *Mary Dollar*. She was sailed to San Francisco, where she remained rotting gently in the Oakland estuary until 1935, when she was renamed *Tango* and turned into an offshore gambling ship. In 1941 she was re-rigged as a six-masted schooner, the second largest six-masted schooner ever commissioned. The next year she left Astoria, Oregon, with a cargo of lumber for South Africa, making a passage by way of the Horn of a hundred and three days. In 1943 she was sold to a Portuguese owner in Durban, and after various misfortunes ended her life in Lisbon in 1946, where she was dismantled – a slow, sad end for one of the most powerful sailing ships ever built.

Kurt's active life was no longer, but much less ignominious. When war was declared in 1914 she sailed from Santa Rosalia for Portland, Oregon, where she was supposed to load lumber for Europe. Instead she laid up in Astoria, where she remained until she was seized when the United States entered the war in 1917. She was then renamed *Dreadnought*, but the name was subsequently changed to *Moshulu* when it was found that many of the new names given to German ships were already in the American registry. The name *Moshulu*, a North American Indian name, was given her by Mrs Woodrow Wilson, the wife of the President, who took upon herself the arduous task of selecting indigenous American names for ex-enemy ships. It was she who bestowed the name *Monongahela* on the unfortunate German barque *Dalbek*.

Between October 1917 and May 1920 *Moshulu* was owned by the United States Shipping Board and for them she made seven voyages from the west coast of North America to Manila and back, and two to Australia, to load wool and chrome. While outward bound in 1920 on the second voyage to Australia she was sold to the newly constituted Moshulu Navigation Company of San Francisco. From Australia she sailed with coal to Manila and then to San Francisco where, in August 1921, she was sold to the Charles Nelson Company of San Francisco for $29,505. She was laid up for nearly a year in San Francisco, until June 1922, when she took a cargo of lumber from Everett, Washington, to Cape Town in eighty-nine days and sailed back from Port Elizabeth to Port Angeles in ballast in a hundred and one.

From January 1924 to April 1927 *Moshulu* was laid up in the Oakland estuary, where so many other sailing ships ended their days; but in June that year she sailed with a cargo of timber from Portland, Oregon, to Williamstown, near Melbourne, by way of the Pacific in eighty-eight days, returning from Geelong to Port Angeles in seventy-five. From February 1928 she was laid up first in Lake Union and then in Winslow, near Seattle, and no one ever thought she would sail again.

In March 1935 Erikson bought her. She was still one of the finest steel barques afloat and he bought her in preference to any other on the west coast on the advice of Boman, one of his trusted captains whom he had sent to the United States for the purpose of buying a strong four-masted barque to replace the full-rigged ship *Grace Harwar*, which had just been scrapped. He paid $12,000 for her, a remarkable bargain even by his standards.

He had her towed to Victoria, British Columbia, where she was cleaned, re-rigged and re-fitted at Yarrow's yard, Esquimalt Harbour, by Boman and thirteen officers and men who were sent out from Finland for the purpose. It was a tremendous undertaking, but when it was completed *Moshulu* was undoubtedly one of the strongest sailing ships left afloat.

On 29 September 1935, *Moshulu* sailed for Spencer Gulf in ballast with a crew of only twenty, five of whom were inexperienced American boys, which allowed only

A Dutch apprentice in *Moshulu*.

six foremast hands in each watch. She went by way of the Pacific and was seventy-six days in passage to Port Lincoln. She loaded grain at Port Victoria and sailed in February 1936 for Queenstown with a crew of twenty-eight, making a passage of a hundred and twelve days. This was not a bad performance for what was virtually a maiden voyage. Of the seventeen ships that sailed from Australia in 1936 only four made passages of under a hundred days, all of them Erikson ships.

For grain ships 1936 was a disastrous year. Erikson's *Herzogin Cecilie* went ashore in the Channel while on passage from Falmouth to Ipswich where she was to discharge her cargo, and eventually became a total loss. *Parma* was so badly damaged while docking in Glasgow that she never sailed again, and *Ponape* was so strained in severe weather off the Horn and in the South Atlantic that she was sold to shipbreakers.

In the autumn of 1937 *Moshulu*, along with two other Erikson ships, loaded timber in the Baltic for Africa, making Copenhagen to Lourenço Marques (now Maputo) in seventy-six days. After discharging her cargo she crossed the Indian Ocean to load grain in Spencer Gulf. She was one of eleven ships to sail from the Gulf in the spring of 1938. She took a hundred and twenty-two days in passage home and others took longer still. In that year *Penang* was partially dismasted in the Tasman Sea and the German *Admiral Karpfanger* (formerly *L'Avenir*) went missing in the Southern Ocean with a crew of sixty including forty cadets.

When I first saw *Moshulu* in Belfast in October 1938 I had never seen a big steel four-masted barque before. All I had seen was a recent photograph of her taken in Belfast Lough in September after her arrival from South Australia. She was lying alongside in the York Dock, waiting for her cargo to be discharged, and even the high scaffolding in Harland & Wolff's shipyard seemed puny by comparison. At that time she was the biggest sailing ship afloat. Her gross weight was 3,116 tons, her length was 320 feet between parallels, her beam was 47 feet and her depth was 28 feet to the main deck.

I had with me a Louis Vuitton trunk, since I had been unable to find a genuine seaman's chest. The trunk had originally been made for some *grande dame* – it had drawers for shoes and a compartment for hanging evening dresses – and it was a bit chic for a Finnish fo'c'sle, with its discreet label, 'Louis Vuitton, Paris, Nice, Vichy'. I had paid £4 for it in a secondhand shop in Hammersmith and it was one of my more successful purchases. I kept tins of jam in the shoe compartments.

Since I was unable to carry the trunk unaided, I took a taxi to the ship, which was only a couple of hundred yards away. As I mounted the gangplank, the masts and yards, yellow ochre in the October sunshine, looked as remote as the North Col of Everest and my legs trembled under me at the thought of going aloft, as I knew I must if I was to become a sailor. On the foredeck stevedores were weighing the sacks as they were winched out through one of the cargo hatches with all the animation of participants in a slow-motion film – a total of 62,153 altogether, 4,878 tons.

One of the crew, a very tough-looking boy called Jansson from the Erikson home port of Mariehamn, slung my trunk on his back unaided and tackled the gangplank like a mountain goat. He was one of the two donkeymen on board who looked after the ship's cargo winches in port.

'Kom,' said Jansson and kicked open the door of what was the starboard fo'c'sle.

Inside it was difficult to see much because of the dense clouds of smoke, but eventually I was able to make out the figures of half a dozen boys, aged between about sixteen and twenty, dressed in blue overalls. They were all sitting at a table which

Moshulu's Third Mate ('Tria') at the jibsheets.

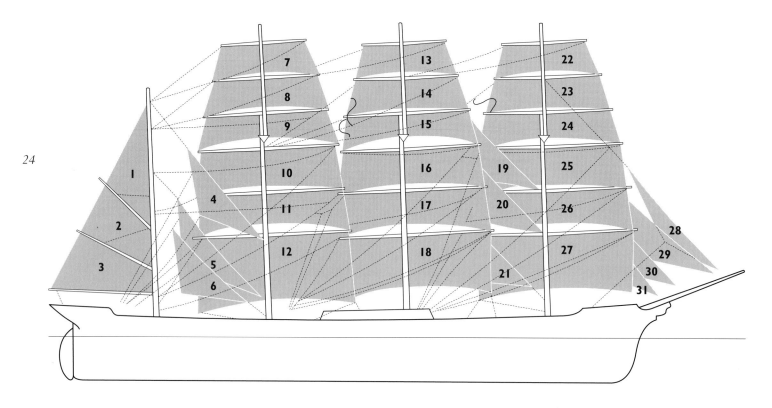

SAIL PLAN OF *MOSHULU*

1. Gaff topsail		18. Mainsail (or main course)
2. Upper spanker		19. Main royal staysail
3. Spanker		20. Main topgallant staysail
4. Jigger topgallant staysail		21. Main topmast staysail
5. Jigger topmast staysail		22. Fore royal
6. Jigger staysail		23. Fore upper topgallant
7. Mizzen royal		24. Fore lower topgallant
8. Mizzen upper topgallant		25. Fore upper topsail
9. Mizzen lower topgallant		26. Fore lower topsail
10. Mizzen upper topsail		27. Foresail (or fore course)
11. Mizzen lower topsail		28. Flying jib
12. Crojack (or crossjack)		29. Outer jib
13. Main royal		30. Inner jib
14. Main upper topgallant		31. Fore topmast staysail
15. Main lower topgallant		
16. Main upper topsail		
17. Main lower topsail		*Mizzen staysails omitted for clarity*

ran more or less the entire length of the fo'c'sle. It had a wooden fiddle round it to stop the crockery sliding on to the deck in rough weather. There were bunks – more like coffins really – on three sides, and everything was painted white or battleship grey. Illumination was by way of half a dozen grimy portholes, and there was an oil lamp suspended in gimbals.

They – the crew – had just finished breakfast and the remains of this ghastly repast, plates of some sort of thick brown stew with macaroni and boiled potatoes in it, were still stacked on the table. The future looked bleak gastronomically speaking. If this was what they were eating in dock in Belfast what was the food going to be like off Cape Horn?

'Good morning,' I said, but they went on staring at me impassively until Jansson, of whom I had already formed a high opinion, poured me some coffee from a large jug and then another boy shoved over a big can of margarine and a loaf of bread, and somehow managed a smile. 'They all drank too bloddy much last night in the Rotterdam Bar,' Jansson said.

I never got to drink or eat anything because at that moment the Second Mate called me out on deck and without preamble ordered me 'Op the rigging!' Like the boys in the fo'c'sle, he had a rather bilious appearance. Perhaps he, too, had been a patron of the Rotterdam Bar.

'Have you ever been in high rigging before?' he asked.

'No, sir.'

'Then get on op!' He was rather impatient. Nevertheless he allowed me to take off my Harris tweed jacket and shirt – I was wearing my best clothes. He wouldn't, however, allow me to change out of my slippery shoes, which were to make things much worse when I got 'op'.

I swung out over the ship's side and started up the first stretch of wooden ratlines to the main top, a roughly semicircular platform with gratings in it. To get on to it I had to climb outwards on the rope ratlines which were seized to steel struts called the futtock shrouds, which braced the top to the mast. It was hard to heave myself on to the top and for a few moments I remained transfixed with my back almost parallel to the deck, like a fly on a ceiling. When I finally got on to the platform I was 82 feet above the heel of the lower mast.

'If you want to live,' the Mate shouted, 'hold on to the shrouds and leave the bloody ratlines alone.'

Below me now was the main yard, 95½ feet long, 2½ feet in diameter and weighing over 5 tons. Like most of the rest of the rigging it was made of steel. The views from this height were impressive.

The next part was nearly 50 feet of vertical rope ratlines seized to the topmast shrouds. Many of them were rotten and one broke when I put my foot on it. The crosstrees when I reached them consisted of an open framework of steel girdering about 130 feet up, which spread the backstays of the royal mast, the highest of all. I stood gingerly on this delicate construction with all Belfast and the Antrim Hills before me, and men who looked like ants on the dockside below.

'Op to the royal yard!' came the imperious voice, fainter now.

There were another 40 feet of trembling topgallant shrouds, past the lower and upper topgallant yards, the ratlines very narrow now and coming to an end altogether just below the royal yard, the highest of all. Now I was ordered 'Op to the mast cap!'. I was pretty well all in emotionally and physically but by now the expected cry of 'Out on the yard!' helped me to haul myself out on to it.

As on all the other yards, an iron rail ran along the top of it. This was a jackstay to which the sail was bent, using rope yarns (robands). In some ships this rail would have another parallel to it to hold on to, since with the sail bent to the jackstay there was little or no handhold. Underneath the yard there was a wire rope which extended the length of it, supported by vertical stirrups. This footrope was called the 'horse' and when I ventured on to it with my slippery shoes I found that my feet skidded away in opposite directions, leaving me like a ballet dancer about to do the splits, hanging grimly on to the jackstay. To test the strength of these 'horses', from time to time they were stretched between two capstans and beaten with capstan bars. If they broke they were replaced. It always seemed a bit unsatisfactory to me. At this point I took off my shoes and socks and jammed them under a jackstay.

Now the Mate told me to 'shin up the main truck to the top of the main mast!' The mast cap was nearly 198 feet above the keel, the last bit 6 feet of bare pole. He told me to sit on the cap but I pretended not to hear. It was higher than Nelson's Column. On the way down he made me go out to the yard-arm of every yard on its weather side. And when I got down on deck he gave me hell for taking my shoes and socks off because they might have fallen on somebody's head and injured them. My flannel trousers were covered with grease from the royal yard tracks, and when I took them to be cleaned in Belfast I found it very expensive. (My pay, like the other apprentices', was to be 100 Finmarks a month – about 10s. Even the Captain, I later discovered, earned only the equivalent of £20, which didn't seem much for such a lonely position of responsibility.)

Apprentices such as myself were bound by the 'Conditions for the Acceptance of Apprentices in Finnish Sailing Vessels'. These stated that they had to be not less than sixteen years of age and of strong constitution. Two doctors' certificates were required, one of which said that the candidate would not be harmed by the work of

Two of my 'brodders', the ship's pigs.

a seaman. Another from a clergyman had to state that the boy was of good moral character. In addition his parents had to pay a premium to the owner of £50 for a year or a round voyage, whichever was the shorter. If he died, a pro-rata repayment of premium was made. That morning in Belfast it seemed to me my father had a very good chance of getting some of his premium back even before the voyage started.

After a few days, however, I could go 'op the rigging' day or night, whatever the weather, almost without feeling afraid, although on one occasion I was blown off a yard in the dark by a sail, and then mercifully blown back on to it. And I never got used to being aloft in an electric storm, which only happened twice during the entire voyage, with St Elmo's Fire burgeoning on the yards.

Then the Second Mate sent me to clean the lavatories which was much worse than going up the rigging at sea. I also looked after the ship's pigs for a week at a time, which was quite fun. 'Your brodders' the Mates used to call them.

Moshulu was no place for the unwary. A tall young man from Massachusetts, George White, who also joined the ship in Belfast, fell into the empty hold through the tonnage opening below No. 3 hatch, hitting the keelson 20 feet below. One of his legs was broken and quite a lot of other things too. He remained in hospital in Belfast until December, two months after we sailed. He was one of the few people who spoke English on board, and I missed him very much. Not long after that a Lithuanian boy, Vytautas Bagdanavicius, fell off the roof of the donkey boiler room and broke his arm.

When *Moshulu's* cargo was finally discharged and we cleaned her out, we found hundreds of mice in the hold. Then we warped up to a lonely quay where we took on 1,500 tons of ballast – rock and sand, part of an old house and, right at the bottom, unknown to us at the time, two dead dogs which the dockers included as 'a joke' and which only really made themselves felt when we began to chuck the ballast overboard in South Australia.

Meanwhile we began to bend sail. Then we went into dry dock. Here you could see *Moshulu*'s fine lines. Unlike most square riggers built at the beginning of the twentieth century, she wasn't slab-sided.

We finally sailed for Port Lincoln, some 15,000 sea miles away, with a crew of 28. The only landfall we were destined to make on this outward voyage was Inaccessible Island, one of the Tristan da Cunha group. The dry dock was filled to the brim and now the men on the dockside raised the caisson and hove it out clear, the dock gates were opened and we passed through them, while men who would soon be sitting down to their dinners strained at great capstans, warping us into the stream. There were no bands, no cheering – only a couple of dozen dockers and the Captain's wife and small son who had come to Ireland from Finland to say goodbye. A voice called 'Good Luck!' but I couldn't make out where it came from, ship or shore. It could have been a prayer offered by any of us. It was the cold, grey drizzly afternoon of 18 October.

An energetic little tug with a red and black funnel took us in tow – the pilot was already aboard *Moshulu* with the Captain, pacing the amidships deck. This was where the chartroom was and from here the Captain could keep an eye on the helmsman. The Captain was called Mikael Sjögren and he had just relinquished command of Erikson's four-masted barque *Archibald Russell*. He was a splendid man and huge.

I knew that at this moment my mother would be watching for us from the house where she was staying with a great friend of hers on the southern shore of the Lough. She had come from England to witness my departure and had been really heroic, but now, here in the gathering darkness, I too shed tears.

Moshulu began to gather way, using the power of the wind for the first time, her topsails, main and mizzen set. It was time for the tug to leave her. The towing cable was cast off and there was a momentary view of the tug, with dark figures hauling frantically at the cable as she turned, her siren giving long blasts of farewell as she faded into the murk astern. I don't know how or when the pilot was dropped. There was too much going on. We went aloft to set a lower topsail. 'Horry up the rigging!' more experienced crew members shouted – I was already beginning to feel fed up with 'Horry ups'. The sail bellied out below and was sheeted home by those on deck.

On that first night and for nights after that, the majority of newly joined boys such as myself didn't know what was happening. Ropes were thrust into our hands for us to haul on and we were made to turn the handles of brace and halliard winches. Many of us couldn't understand the orders, which were mostly in pretty technical maritime Swedish. Between 6 p.m. and 5 a.m. we tacked ship three times, which needed all hands. To tack ship meant putting *Moshulu* about by bringing her head across the wind, a tricky thing to do at night with a green crew.

At four in the morning a horribly insistent voice bellowed 'Rise op! Rise op!' in my ear and I woke to find that it was all hands on deck to tack ship. *Moshulu* was now going about for the second time, an operation which was still pretty mystifying because of the darkness. I was consigned to haul a rope with five or six others behind the senior donkeyman ('Doonkey 1'), a savage-looking but likeable man wearing a cloth cap.

Doonkey encouraged us with the most extraordinary noises: 'Hor vaay. . .oooha. . . . Han or han . . . Eeor . . . Eeeor . . . Curm . . . urp' and lastly 'Slack oop' which indicated that 'Doonkey' was about to belay, or make fast. At this everyone on the rope let go of it, except myself who ended up banging my head in the scuppers.

'Name of Sarrtan! Was slack oop,' said 'Doonkey'. (I soon discovered that 'Sarrtan' was the equivalent of 'Blast' or 'Hell' in English.)

At 5 a.m. I was placed on the fo'c'sle head by the Third Mate ('Tria') for *utkik* (lookout). 'Two bells, vessel to port. Three bells, vessel ahead. One bell, vessel to starboard,' he intoned, sounding a bit like a bell himself, and vanished.

The *Moshulu* was rippling through the water now at about 5 knots. It was a dark night. Almost immediately I thought I saw the lights of a vessel to starboard and struck two bells with laborious care, instead of one, and remained trembling at the possible consequences. Tria appeared like lightning to tell me that there was no ship to starboard but that there was another much closer ahead that I should have noticed.

By six in the morning I was sure that I was going to be seasick, but wasn't. A lot of people were, including the Captain, but at least he could retire to his quarters, which included a lavatory. Taanila, a small Finnish boy, was sick continuously for five days, which was a great bore for him and anyone working to leeward of him up in the rigging.

For five days we staggered about the Irish Sea, now beating up to the coast of Wicklow, now fetching up on the other tack by the South Stack Light on the Welsh side. We tacked ship so many times that I lost count. I had never been so tired in my entire life and none of the newly joined crew had either. We were far too done in to appreciate the pyramids of gleaming white sails towering above us.

In the watch below I would collapse into a dreamless sleep until the dreadful cries of whoever was *påpass* (pronounced 'porpuss'), the fag to the officer of the watch who had blown three whistles, announced that we were going to tack or wear ship. Either of these operations required all hands on deck, including the Sailmaker and the Assistant Sailmaker, the Carpenter, the two Donkeymen, the Steward, the Cook and the Steward's Boy. And the Captain and his three Mates, and the rest of us.

While I was engaged in these operations I felt like a somnambulist, but without the somnambulist's happy facility for not tripping over things. I was forever catching my toe on ringbolts – steering cables which were connected with the steering wheels amidships by wire cables running through sheaves in the 130-foot-long after deck to the poop, underneath which were a pair of auxiliary wheels. This was in case the cables parted and *Moshulu* was left helmless, which she sometimes was.

During these nights in the Irish Sea the Mates, all three of them, were very jumpy. They had reason to be. In 1938 steamer look-outs were quite likely to miss seeing a big, engineless barque with only port and starboard lights and no masthead light. And we saw plenty of steamers in the course of the next five days and nights.

By Saturday the Captain gave up trying to beat down the Irish Sea and out into the Western Approaches and headed back past the mouth of Belfast Lough, hoping to reach the Atlantic by way of the North Channel. By supper time on Saturday – we had sailed on Tuesday – there was no more fresh food, except for a few cabbage leaves in which meat balls were wrapped. Our numbers, however, had been augmented by two robins and a thrush. They had arrived on board exhausted on Wednesday but had soon become cheeky and started to steal food from the ships' chickens, which were by now thoroughly demoralized.

That night I stood my first wheel from 10 to 11 o'clock at night. In fact only the first three minutes were solo. In that time I succeeded in putting *Moshulu* completely off course, swinging her through north-east to north-north-east until from aloft came a terrifying crashing of canvas, block and chain-sheets as *Moshulu* came into the wind. I spent the next fifty-seven minutes under tuition from an Anglophobe able seaman called Sedelquist, who told me I was 'like English rosbif. No focking good.' And the First Mate, officer of the watch, got a rocket from the Captain for allowing me to go to the wheel alone on a dark night. We were near the mouth of the Clyde by this time and the place was lousy with shipping.

On Sunday morning a big orange sun came up from behind low ramparts of black cloud and revealed a peaceful scene. The barque was landlocked on three sides, ghosting along with her topgallants set, her sails aflame in the sunlight. To the north were the islands of Jura and Islay, to the south-east the lonely extremity of the Mull of Kintyre.

Sunday was a free day in the ship, apart from sailing her and taking in or setting sails, and after breakfast the ship's only gramophone was removed from the starboard fo'c'sle and taken to the port fo'c'sle where it immediately expired. However Jansson repaired it and throughout the afternoon the dreadful sounds of the 'Post Horn Gallop' and 'In a Little Dutch Mill' (*Moshulu*'s only records) floated across the still waters of the North Channel on which, apart from the south-easterly set of the stream, we were utterly becalmed. The crew lay on the hatch covers and we let the October sun warm us. Twice I was called away with the port watch to clew up the course sails to save them slatting and banging, and later to brace the yards.

Towards evening a breeze sprang up, the still waters began to heave and the ship began to lift to the long fetch of the Atlantic swell. At once the courses were sheeted home and in the gathering dusk the ship began to move out of the North Channel. That night the wind freshened from the south-west. By midnight *Moshulu* was running at 13 knots and flinging out a 60-foot bow wave on either side of her. At supper-time we all banged our plates and sang with sheer joy, and at the change of watch we took the upper topgallants off her as she was running heavily. And from aloft came the great roaring sound that I heard now for the first time, and will perhaps never hear again, of strong winds in the rigging of a big ship. The Atlantic swallowed the *Moshulu* and her crew. From now on we received no authentic news from the outside world. The Second Mate was said to have a radio but no one knew if it worked. The ship had no wireless. We could have been at war without knowing it.

I must have had some premonition that war, when it came, would mean the end of the big sailing ships working in the Australian grain trade, and the way of life of the men and boys who sailed in them, for I had brought my camera with me. It was a Zeiss Super Ikonta – a tiny, folding, bellows camera with an F3.5 Tessar lens, a Compur shutter and a coupled rangefinder, which took sixteen pictures on 3¼ x 2¼ inch roll film. I didn't have an exposure meter but by using something known as a Burroughs Wellcome Exposure Calculator, which came in the back of a diary, I got some surprisingly good results, considering how little I knew then, and know now for that matter, about photography.

Being an apprentice, I took nearly all the photographs in this book during my free watches, many of them when I was done-in after long hours on deck, at the wheel or up in the rigging. It required an effort of will not to go to sleep as soon as I went below, but to turn out again with the camera. For obvious reasons there are few if any pictures of the ship when all hands were called to take in sail, tack or wear her round, bring her to anchor or get her under way from the anchorage. Such moments, as any yachtsman knows, are inimical to photography. Once, when I was on deck during a fearful storm in the Southern Ocean, a huge wave reared over the rail, and I was too late to protect my camera. As I opened it in the fo'c'sle I was in an agony of dread, but though the camera was wet the film was undamaged.

Anyone who wishes to know more of the story behind the photographs will find it in *The Last Grain Race*, a narrative account of the voyage and of my time aboard *Moshulu*, which I wrote in the 1950s and which is still in print today.

Looking back it seems to me a pity that none of the great photographers who were at work between the wars made a round voyage in one of the grain or nitrate ships. If there had been anything like the number of young professional photographers that there are today, one or two would surely have done so. But the great photographers of the 1930s were otherwise engaged. The best of them were either busy in Europe recording a way of life that was about to perish for ever, or else they were at the battle front of one of the minor wars that were a prelude to the big one. Besides, few could afford the time for a round trip that took a minimum of eight months and, if there were delays in getting a cargo or the passage itself was a long one, could easily take a year or more.

Some of the pictures I had developed in Australia, and the rest were developed when I got home. My camera was a wartime casualty. In 1942 I took a great many photographs on the coast of Syria, where life was still very primitive. When I was captured, the authorities in Malta went through my baggage before sending it on to my next of kin, and I never saw those pictures or my Super Ikonta again.

35

Apprentice greasing the wire braces.

 *Moshulu* as I first saw her on a cold October morning in 1938, lying alongside in York Dock, Belfast. At that time she was the biggest sailing ship in the world, and she made even the scaffolding at Harland & Wolff's shipyard seem puny.

 ▶ The gangplank was steep and I kept slipping backwards as I struggled with my trunk. Then a very tough-looking boy called Jansson appeared, slung it on his back and swarmed up the gangplank with it like some great primate.

◀ The masts and yards, shining yellow ochre in the sunshine, looked as remote as the North Col and my legs trembled under me at the thought of going aloft, as I knew I must if I was to be a sailor.

▶ 'Have you ever been in high rigging before?' the Second Mate asked me almost as soon as I was on board. 'No, sir.' 'Then get on op.' I could scarcely believe my ears. The mast cap, which was nearly 198 feet above the keel, was higher than Nelson's Column.

40

I started towards the rigging from the side nearest the quay but a cry from the Mate stopped me in my tracks. '*Babord*, port side. Better to fall into the dock than on to the quay.' By the time I was down again my best flannel trousers were covered in grease and I was pretty well all in emotionally.

While we were in port we went over the side every morning to chip rust and red lead the shell plating – these men are in a hazardous position below the outflow of the lavatories. On the first day I unwittingly let slip a clove-hitch and tilted the precarious platform, spilling the red lead and dropping my hammer. I was told that the cost of the hammer would be deducted from my pay, which was 10s a month.

Working on the bowsprit

Moshulu was still discharging her cargo of grain from South Australia. Stevedores were weighing the sacks as they came out of Number One cargo hatch on the foredeck.

► After the cargo was discharged we warped up to a lonely quay where we took on 1,500 tons of ballast for the outward voyage to Australia. This consisted of sand, most of an old house and two dead dogs which the dockers in Belfast included 'as a joke'.

44

 After discharging the cargo we went into dry dock. Here you could see *Moshulu*'s lines. Unlike most square-riggers built at the end of the nineteenth century she was not slab-sided.

▶ Bending a foresail ready for the voyage. For winter in the Atlantic we needed a complete set of thirty-one storm sails, and there was tremendous confusion about finding them in the darkness between decks.

▲ A single little red and black tug took us in tow up the Lough towards the Irish Sea.

◀ We sailed from Belfast for South Australia on the cold dreary afternoon of 18 October, 1938, with a crew of twenty-eight. The dry dock was filled, and men who would soon be sitting snug at home strained at great capstans, warping us out into the stream. I heard some-one shout 'Good luck'.

▶ We made sail in the last of the light. Ropes were thrust into my hands and I hauled on them, though I had no idea what I was doing.

48

The Mates chose their watches. To my dismay I was put in the port watch with most of the younger Finns — a turbulent lot who spoke hardly any English.

The port and starboard watches.

◀ Both port and starboard fo'c'sles had twelve berths, only ten of which were occupied, the other two being loaded with sea chests and gear. In the centre was a long table which was used for eating, playing games and doing the washing-up — a ghastly job.

▶ When I first saw John Sömmarström, *Moshulu*'s Sailmaker and the Assistant Bosun, he was sitting in his shirtsleeves reading *The Seven Pillars of Wisdom* — he spoke fluent English with a Scots accent and was extremely well read. He'd spent forty-three of his fifty-eight years at sea, all of them in sail, and because of his exceptional experience he earned about £7 a month.

51

52 It took us five days of
    tacking up and down
    the Irish Sea to get out
    into the North Atlantic
    by way of the North
    Channel. Then on the
    night of 24 October,
    the wind came up
    from the south-west
    and *Moshulu* ran
    13 knots under
    upper topgallants.

◀ From aloft came the great roaring sound, that I heard now for the first time and will perhaps never hear again, of strong winds in the rigging of a big ship.

▶ Two of the *'matros'* or able seamen putting a seizing on the main stay. Like all the other standing rigging it was of steel wire. The sail set on it was the main topmast staysail.

Clewing up the main
royal while the Captain
looks aloft.

The starboard watch
haul on the mizzen
royal halliard to raise
the yard. The mizzen
course sheet is led to
the capstan.

◄ On our first Saturday at sea we washed down the paintwork on the main deck.

▶ We also painted the lighthouses on the fo'c'sle head which protected the port and starboard lights.

'Yonny Valker', an apprentice who genuinely believed the world was flat, eating his breakfast outside the galley. We all dreamt constantly of food.

◀ Apprentice Newby
doing the washing-up,
using half a kerosene can
of hot seawater. Fifty
minutes were allowed for
doing the job for all three
foc's'les and everything
had to be spotless, what-
ever the weather. We did
it a week at a time.
Cleaning the lavatories
was far preferable.

61

Mikelsonn, a Danish
apprentice from the
schoolship *Danmark.*

Washing-up was
hardest in the fo'c'sle
with the watch below,
who were often using
the table to play a noisy
card game called
Bismarck.

Twelve days out, on 30 October, we were about 500 miles west of the coast of Portugal. Between noon on the 25th and the 27th the wind was strong from the west and we sailed 496 miles. On Sunday, now that there was no more fresh water to spare, we washed our clothes in seawater on the foredeck and cut one another's hair.

▶ The *Timmerman*, or Carpenter, was the strongest man on the ship. During the voyage he had twenty-four teeth out at one sitting.

A close shave: the Lithuanian apprentice, Vytautas Bagdanavicius, having a haircut.

► Bending the mizzen lower topgallant to the jackstay with robands made with teased rope yarns.

◄ Twenty-two days out we began to send down the storm canvas and bend old, patched fair-weather sails in order to preserve the good stuff. A complete set of thirty-one sails cost, at that time, about £2,500. The main course sail measured 88 feet on the head and weighed over a ton.

Twenty-four days out
we picked up the
North-East Trades
about 150 miles off Rio
de Oro on the north
west African coast.
Here the mainsail is
being bent and the
man on the weather
yard-arm is hauling out
the head of the sail and
reeving the head earing
to a hook on the yard.

Sending aloft and bending a royal 160 feet up, while standing on the footrope or 'horse'. These footropes were tested by being stretched between two capstans and beaten with an iron bar – if they broke they were replaced.

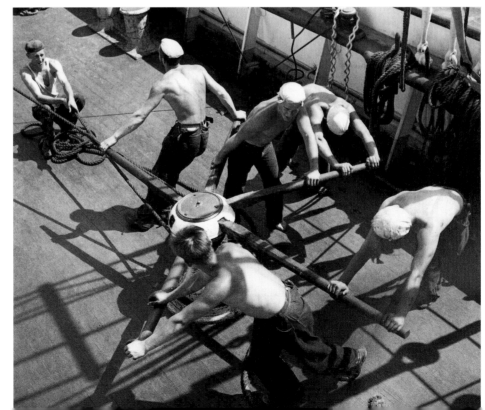

70 *Moshulu*'s Captain, Mikael Sjögren, was a huge and splendid man who had previously commanded Erikson's four-masted barque *Archibald Russell*. She too was now bound for Spencer Gulf.

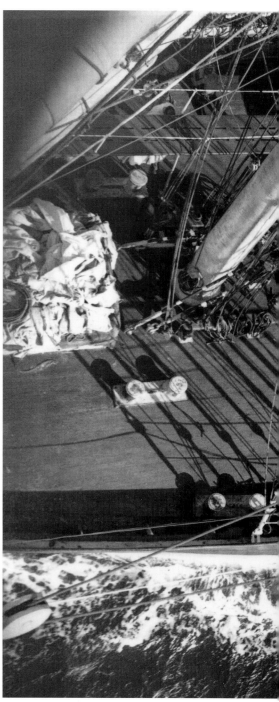

The bridge deck seen from aloft in the mizzen rigging.

The Danish apprentice
Mikelsonn at the wheel
on the amidships bridge
deck. The twin wheels
were connected with the
steering gear under the
poop by wire cables
which ran in sheaves.
Sometimes these cables
broke in heavy weather,
and then a similar pair of
auxiliary wheels under
the poop had to be
connected to the steering
quadrant, and manned –
very quickly.

As the weather grew warmer thousands of bedbugs swarmed in the fo'c'sle bunks, so my friend Jack Kroner and I made hammocks from old rotten canvas which we begged from the Sailmaker. Mine crashed to the deck within seconds of being completed, and eventually the Sailmaker gave me his old one in exchange for 3 ounces of tobacco.

73

▼ Members of the starboard watch playing chess.

74 The Assistant Sailmaker with a small model of *Moshulu*. Several of the crew made models, which were much prized – the Second Mate had sold a large one of *Moshulu* for £60 in Belfast.

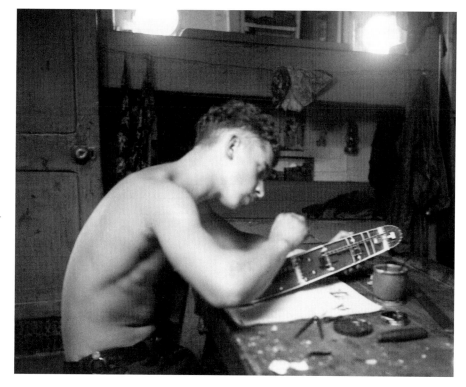

Vytautas Bagdanavicius, and *below* Sedelquist, an able seaman who had served in the *Herzogin Cecilie* on her last voyage.

76 Off duty: one of the
able seamen, Sandell,
wearing a hat, with the
Head Donkeyman
behind him and *right*
the Steward's Boy.

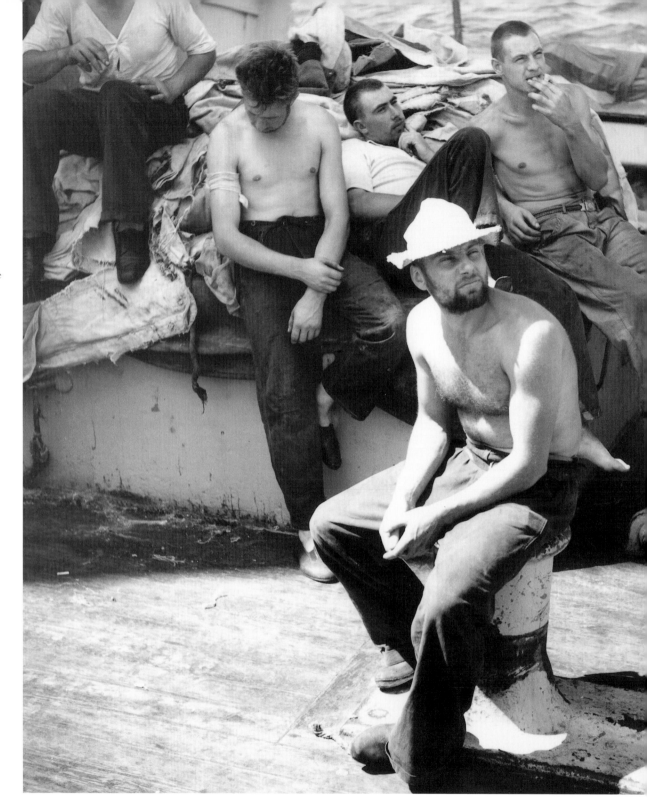

▼ The Sailmaker was a
famous figure in the
Erikson ships — a great
man who put heart into
us when we were all in.

◄ Twenty-eight days out, nine degrees north of the Equator, we lost the North-East Trades and spent five days in the Doldrums. At 4 a.m. on the morning of the sixth day we were woken by a series of explosions – the sound of six sails blowing out as a tornado hit the ship, catching her in full sail. The noise on deck, with screaming wind and beating canvas, was indescribable. *Left,* the tattered foresail.

▶ Sending up a new foresail. After the tornado there were heaps of torn canvas everywhere. Thirty-two days out we picked up the South-East Trades in 4°N, 22° W. In the previous twenty-four hours we had only sailed 76 miles. In the next four days we sailed 931.

80 We crossed the Equator on Monday, 21 November in Longtitude 29°W. On Tuesday we all stopped work for the initiation ceremony – a pretty rough affair during which a disgusting pudding of dough, engine oil and nutmeg was forced down the throats of the initiates by the Second Mate, dressed as a 'Surgeon'.

▶ After that we were coated from head to foot in red lead, Stockholm tar and white paint, and the Sydkryss – the Southern Cross – was shaved on to our scalps and picked out in green paint. Everyone got drunk and sporadic fighting broke out.

▼ Meanwhile the 'Chaplain', in a long oilskin coat and paper top hat, read us a somewhat unusual lesson.

▲ Afterwards we got the worst of the paint off with paraffin and sand, but we were still very sore.

◀ Finding two enamel bowls of equal size to upholster Neptune's sinister wife held up the proceedings.

Next day we lay around licking our wounds . . . and playing Bismarck.

▶ Meantime the work of the ship continued. Here an apprentice is overhauling buntlines on the fore course. The buntlines were used for drawing the sail up to the yard for furling. When the sail was set and sheeted home, enough line had to be hauled up through the bunt-blocks on the yard and stopped with easily breakable seizings to leave some slack at the bunt and prevent chafing.

◀ Thirty-six days out the Brazilian penal colony of Fernando Noronha was abeam, some 80 miles to starboard. By now all the experienced seamen had been taken off watch and made 'daymen' – either helping the Sailmaker to mend sails or else reeving new running rigging or splicing ratlines.

▶ Apprentices like me were sent aloft in bosun's chairs to paint the shrouds or grease the wire braces with a mixture of oil and tallow. These were terrifying jobs since the greatest crime was to drop paint or grease on the deck.

86

We lost the South-East Trades in 23°S. Two days later the wind had shifted ENE and *Moshulu* began to go.

From noon to noon on 3 and 4 December, with the wind first ENE, Force 3 to 4, and later NE, Force 6, she logged 333 sea miles and made 315 between observed positions. Between noon and midnight on 4 December she logged 168 miles.

Taking in the upper topgallants.

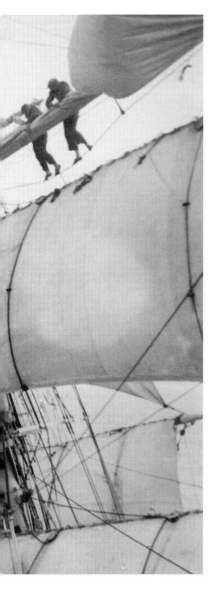

▶ On the morning of 5 December we reset the upper topgallants and the main and mizzen courses which we had taken in at ten o'clock the previous night. In the evening of that day, just as the sun was setting, we made our first landfall, Inaccessible Island, 20 miles WSW of Tristan da Cunha, 1,700 miles W of the African mainland and 1,800 miles E of the coast of South America.

◄ The lonely peak of Inaccessible Island, 6,700 feet high, was clothed in dark cloud, and on the water between the ship and the land thousands of seabirds hovered or floated. Inaccessible Island was entirely uninhabited and the sense of desolation was tremendous.

►Furling in the main royal. On 13 December, 56 days out, we crossed the longitude of the Cape of Good Hope in 40°S and entered the Southern Indian Ocean. There was a big sea running.

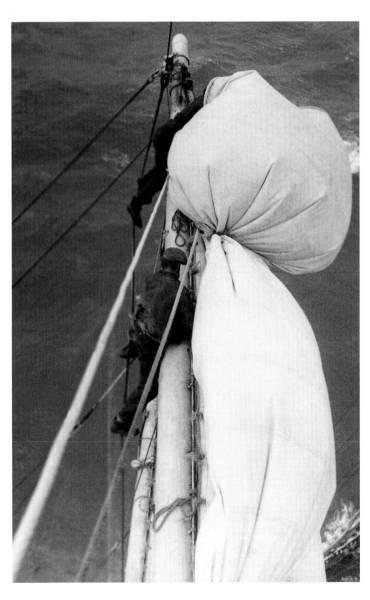

92

◀ Sheeting home the fore topgallant staysail.

▶ Taking in the fore topgallant staysail. This was the most dangerous place to work in the whole ship. The steel bowsprit was 69 feet long and there was no safety netting beneath it.

94

◀ The starboard watch trimming the yards on the main mast.

▶ One of the three Jarvis brace winches which were used to brace the yards. Previously the job would have taken ten men hauling on a rope, but a Jarvis brace winch got it done with only half that number. Course yard braces wound on to the forward drums, nearest the camera, lower topsail braces to the centre ones, upper topsail braces to the aftermost drums.

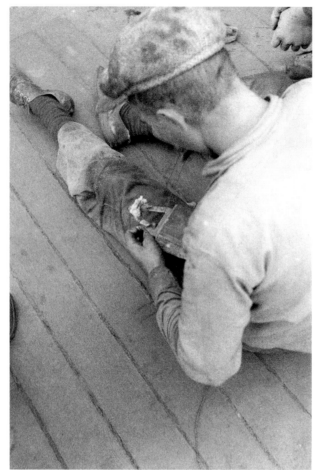

96 Forty degrees south, in what are known as the Roaring Forties, albatross were with us constantly. One of the crew devised a trap consisting of a hollow triangle of brass with a cork float, which he baited with a piece of dried fish and threw over the side. An albatross caught its beak in the trap and we hauled it aboard, not realizing that when we returned it to the sea it might drown.

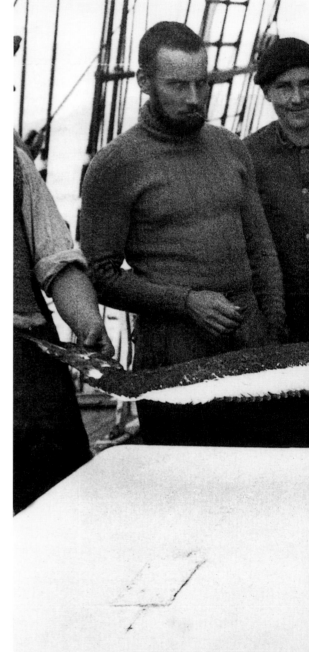

The albatross, posed for pictures on the coaming of the after wheelhouse. Its wingspan tip to tip was at least 11 feet.

◀ On the seventy-seventh day out we entered the Great Australian Bight, and on 7 January, at 4 a.m., we made a landfall at Cape Catastrophe, to the west of the entrance to Spencer Gulf. After beating about to leeward for a day and a night we finally anchored by Boston Island, 8 miles offshore from Port Lincoln, at three in the afternoon. We had been at sea for eighty-two days and had sailed 15,000 sea miles. *Passat* had already arrived on 24 December from Copenhagen and was still waiting for a cargo.

▲ *Lawhill* arrived next day, eighty-five days out from Birkenhead — a great passage for an old ship built in 1892.

Moshulu, seen from the rowing boat in which we visited *Passat*. Her Captain gave us grim news. There were no freights, and we might have to wait for months.

100

▶ The Captain's launch, in which he disappeared while we mouldered on board. Rumour had it that he was enjoying a series of parties with the other captains.

▶ Hanging about off Port Lincoln. It was a week before we were allowed ashore. A terrible wind blew down the Gulf from the deserts of the interior and the temperature in the shade was 114°.

On Saturday we were
finally allowed to row
the eight miles in to
Port Lincoln. We had
no money in our
pockets, for the
Captain had wisely
withheld our pay in
case we deserted the
ship — which was not
unknown — and for a
while I stood on the
long jetty wondering
what to do.

102

▲ In two days we
got rid of 300 tons
of ballast.

◀ After two weeks
at this exposed and
inhospitable anchorage
news came that
Erikson's London
agents had secured us a
freight, and we began
to get rid of the ballast,
slinging it over the side
in wicker baskets.

▼ After six and a half days we made sail for Port Victoria on the other side of the Gulf with half the ballast still on board, discharging it as we went. At Port Victoria we finally uncovered what remained of the dogs.

▲ In the hold the temperature went up to 120° and the two dead dogs buried somewhere near the bottom began to make themselves felt.

 Flaked out after our efforts in the hold. We lay at Port Victoria for a month and two days.

▶ *Olivebank*, *Pamir*, *Pommern*, *Viking* and *Moshulu* at Port Victoria, February 1939. The great concourse of commercial square riggers gathered there that spring was the last the world would ever see.

106

Pamir, in the foreground,
and *Moshulu* at Port
Victoria.

▶ *Pommern* sailing in
from the ballast grounds
at Port Victoria.

108

▶ 'Port Veek', as the
boys from the ships
called it, was a one-
street town, and that
street was unsurfaced.

▲ An inhabitant giving
a crank to one of 'Port
Veek's few cars.

▲ Kneebone's Café, where most of the crews went when they got ashore. We all had one thing in common: we were practically penniless and permanently hungry.

◄ A 'liddle trink' too many for one of the crew. Fortunately we enjoyed a good deal of hospitality.

110

▲ Grain was Port Victoria's reason for existence. There were sacks of it everywhere.

▶ John Scott-Todd, Erikson's agent, without whom I would have had a hungry time of it.

▶ The main jetty at Port Victoria – almost exactly the same then as it is today. The grain was run out on a light railway to where the ketches waited to take it out to the ships.

▲ Some of us were
tempted to desert to
the ketches, where the
pay was much better,
but no one did.

◀ *Viking* was the first ship to sail for Europe, leaving Port Victoria on 16 February. From Spencer Gulf it was 6,000 miles to Cape Horn. Thirteen ships sailed from the Gulf in the spring of 1939 of which ten — *Passat, Pommern, Pamir, Lawhill, Viking, Archibald Russell, Winterhude, Olivebank, Killoran* and *Moshulu* — belonged to Gustav Erikson. The others were *Padua, Abraham Rydberg* and *Kommodore Johnsen.*

◀ *Moshulu* sailed for Queenstown (now Cobh) in the Irish Republic at 6.30 a.m. on Saturday 11 March. A man — scarcely visible here against the foam — was put over the side to strop and secure the anchors to the hook of the anchor crane. Then we put them to bed on the poop.

113

114

◀ By evening the wind was rising in the north-west and the glass fell rapidly. Here the boys on the yard are beginning to take in the royals. Soon we were in the middle of a spectacular electric storm which literally made my hair stand on end.

▶ As we drove south-east at 12 knots across the mouth of the Bass Strait, west of Tasmania, constant bracing was needed because the wind kept shifting. Soon we saw our first wandering albatross. It was difficult to believe that a day and a night away to the north of us were bungalows with red tin roofs, and cinemas, and men who visited their girlfriends on motorbikes.

116

◀ For part of the voyage I was given the job of looking after the ship's pigs, which lived in sties by the fo'c'sle head – 'dose brodders of yours' as the First Mate called them. There were three black males – Fabian, Filimon and Auguste – and a large white female who never had a name. She was eaten before we reached Cape Horn.

▶ On 24 March, thirteen days out, we crossed the 180th meridian. There was a huge sea running. At 5.30 next morning we took in the upper topgallants, and by noon *Moshulu* had sailed 296 miles in 23½ hours – the best day's run with cargo she ever made for Erikson.

118

◀ The glass fell steadily. We took in the mizzen and main courses in heavy hail with the wind WSW, Force 8. It was freezing and we had a fearful time with the wildly swinging yard.

▶ Storm blowing up in the Southern Ocean. There were two men at the wheel constantly now.

▲ It was damp and cold in the fo'c'sles and the best place to be was in one's bunk. This is Hörglund, one of the able seamen, about to turn in.

◀ The only illumination was from a paraffin lamp.

Making fast the mizzen upper topsail in a Force 9. The strength of the wind and the waves was awe-inspiring. *Moshulu* seemed a mere speck as she was driven across the greatest uninterrupted expanse of water in the world.

◀ The waves were like great black walls of water, a quarter of a mile apart and as high as a three-storey house.

▼ The noise was indescribable
– the shrieking of the wind in
the shrouds, the clanging of
freeing ports, and the thunder
of the sea as it came over the
rail like a mill race.

▶ The wind rose even higher. A lesser ship might well have foundered, but *Moshulu* ran before the storm.

▲ The wave that gave my camera a bath. Amazingly, though wet the camera still continued to function – but less well.

One of the crew, washed into the scuppers.

126 We no longer cared
that we were wet, only
leaping for the lifelines
when we were in
danger of being washed
overboard.

The main and bridge decks
seen from the main yard-arm.
From time to time the whole
deck would disappear under
water, and then *Moshulu*
would rise up again.

▶ Hanging on for dear life.

130

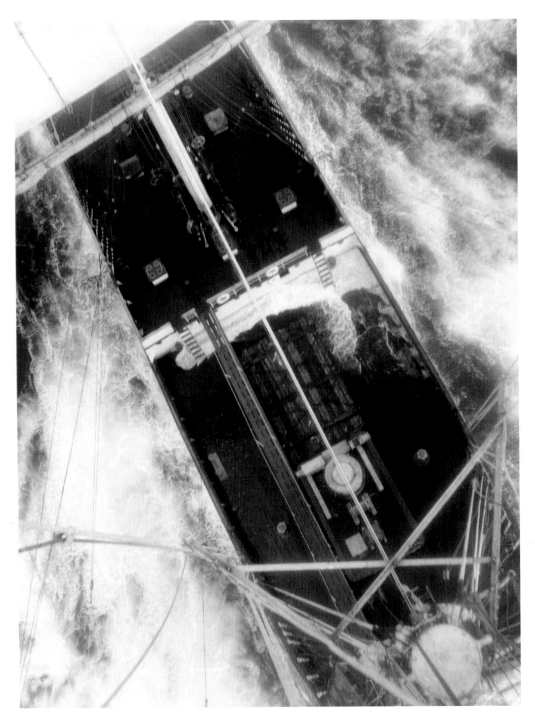

◀ The foredeck photographed from the fore royal yard at the height of the gale.

▶ Wind WSW, Force 11, fifteen days out from Port Victoria. *Moshulu* was still taking huge seas aboard. Looking aft from the fore yard-arm.

◀ The storm enters its last phase. An apprentice goes aloft to overhaul buntlines in the main rigging.

By noon on 26 March the barometer was rising steadily, and by 9 p.m. the wind had fallen though there was still a tremendous sea running. At two in the morning we re-set the royals and within an hour or two we were once more in full sail. Between midnight on Tuesday 28 March and midnight on Wednesday *Moshulu* logged 297 miles with the wind Force 6 to 8. Wednesday 29th was the toughest, coldest night of the voyage and the Captain issued us all with rum. We queued up outside the charthouse to receive our dollops, which we took from a big wooden spoon.

133

134

◀ On Easter Sunday, 9 April, we sighted *Passat* in 56°S, 74°W, 15 miles away from us on the port beam. She had left Port Lincoln two days before us and there was tremendous excitement. Now the voyage became a race. Our Captain ordered the royals to be set, and Captain Lindvall of *Passat* immediately set royals, mainsail and topmast staysails. By four in the afternoon she had fallen far astern, and when she disappeared from view in a squall it was the last we saw of her. On Bank Holiday Monday we passed Cape Horn, though we were too far south to see anything but the distant snow-covered peaks of the Diego Ramirez Islands.

◀ The two surviving pigs, Fabian and Filimon, rounding Cape Horn. During the storm Filimon, believing the ship was about to founder, had charged the barricade of hatch covers, intent on finding a place in the boats.

▶ A week after we rounded the Horn the weather grew warmer and we began to bend fair-weather canvas. At 3 a.m. on the 22nd, in torrential rain, the ship was struck by a *Pampero*, a fearful south-westerly wind which came off the South American coast, and the fore upper topgallant blew out. Later that day we picked up the South-East Trades, losing them ten days later 4° south of the Line in the Doldrums.

◀ Swimming in the Doldrums.

▲ Twenty-five days from the Horn we crossed the Equator in 29°W, still with a chance to beat *Parma*'s record passage of eighty-three days in 1933. Next day we caught a shark, but we were all somewhat relieved when it straightened the hook and got away. I vowed I would never swim off the ship again.

◀ North of the Line the wind dropped, leaving us wallowing on the outward extremities of the Sargasso Sea. On 23 May we logged only 10 miles between noon and 8 p.m. and tempers became frayed — especially the First Mate's.

138

◀ Seventy-five days out we began to see some shipping. One of the steamers, *Brasilien*, reported us at Lloyd's.

▶ By 1 June, eighty-two days out, we had lost hope of beating *Parma*'s record. In five days we only sailed 235 miles.

◀ On 7 June, 150 miles to Queenstown, the wind came back from the north-east and later the north, and we made 9 knots on the port tack. At five in the afternoon the fore royal blew out.

▶ On 8 June we were 80 miles from the Irish coast, and we could smell land. At 8 p.m. we raised the Fastnet Rock 15 miles to the north-east, but then the wind dropped and we were becalmed until 5 a.m. on the 10th, when the wind shifted and we squared away for Queenstown. At 11 a.m. the pilot cutter appeared and guided us into the roads. News spread that we were first home, beating *Passat* and our most formidable rival *Padua*. The race was won.

'Coming again?' the Captain asked me, as he signed my discharge – by now I was a *'lättmatros'* or ordinary seaman.

'I'll think it over,' I said. But within a few months war began to disperse the Erikson fleet.

The first casualty was *Olivebank*, sunk in September 1939 in a German minefield with the loss of her captain and thirteen of her crew. But it was not yet the end for *Moshulu*. From Queenstown she was towed to Glasgow, where she discharged her cargo, and where I left the ship. In October 1939, with Captain Sjögren still in command, she sailed from Gothenburg for Buenos Aires, where she loaded grain and sailed for Norway in January 1940. By the time she reached Farsund in May, Norway was already under German occupation, and she was seized by the Germans and ordered to Kristiansand to discharge her cargo. She reached the port on 22 May. This was her last commercial voyage.

The only member of the crew who remained aboard her was the Sailmaker, John Sömmarström. The rest returned to Finland, which by this time was at war with Russia. *Moshulu* remained at Kristiansand until March 1942, when the Germans had her towed to the Oslo fjord. There, at Horten, she was rigged down and her masts and yards taken ashore.

After this the Sailmaker returned to Finland. From Horten *Moshulu* was taken in tow for Kirkenes and went aground on passage but was refloated. Eventually she reached the Lofoten Islands, where she remained until September 1947, when she broke her moorings and ran ashore in a gale. In May 1948 she was refloated, and her hull was bought by a Miss Jacobsen of Narvik for nearly twice as much as Erikson had paid for her in 1935. After that she was sold to another Norwegian buyer, and was used as a grain store in Stockholm until 1952.

Back in port after ninety-one days at sea. The port watch celebrate with some Irish visitors.

In that year she was bought by Heinz Schliewen, a German shipowner who had already bought *Pamir* and *Passat* from Belgian shipbreakers. He intended to re-rig her completely and use her as a cargo-carrying cadet ship, but the cost was prohibitive. In 1953 he sold her to a Swedish firm to be used once more as a grain store, and that November she was again towed to Stockholm.

She remained as a grain store for the next seventeen years, purchased by the Finnish Government in 1961 in exchange for 3,200 tons of Russian rye and towed to Naantali in Finland. In 1970, she was bought by the American Speciality Restaurants Corporation, rigged out in Holland and towed to New York.

From there *Moshulu* was moved to Penn's Landing, Philadelphia, where she was used as a restaurant until she was damaged by fire in 1989. In 1994 she was purchased by HMS Ventures Inc. and restored in the style of a turn-of-the-century luxury liner. Today she is a restaurant and tourist attraction on the Philadelphia waterfront, moored at Pier 34.

	OUTWARD 1938				HOMEWARD 1939			
SHIP AND CAPTAIN	SAILED	ARRIVED	DAYS		SAILED	ARRIVED	DAYS	DISCHARGED
Moshulu / Sjögren 4-masted barque	Belfast 18 Oct	Port Lincoln 8 Jan	82		Port Victoria 11 March	Queenstown 10 June	91	Glasgow
Padua / Wendt 4-masted barque	Valparaiso 14 Jan	Port Lincoln 8 March	53		Port Lincoln 3 April	Fastnet 5 July	93	Glasgow (96)
Pamir / Björkfelt 4-masted barque	Gothenburg 24 Sept	Port Victoria 24 Dec	91		Port Victoria 8 March	Falmouth 12 June	96	Southampton
Passat / Lindvall 4-masted barque	Copenhagen 24 Sept	Port Lincoln 24 Dec	91		Port Lincoln 9 March	Lizard 15 June	98	Belfast
Pommern / Broman 4-masted barque	Belfast 24 Sept	Port Victoria 11 Dec	78		Port Victoria 20 March	Falmouth 15 July	117	Hull
Olivebank / Granith 4-masted barque	Greenock 28 Oct	Port Victoria 2 Feb	97		Port Victoria 20 March	Queenstown 17 July	119	Barry
Archibald Russell / Sommarlund 4-masted barque	Falmouth 5 Nov	Port Lincoln 2 Feb	89		Port Germein 3 April	Falmouth 2 August	121	Hull
Viking / Morn 4-masted barque	Copenhagen 28 Sept	Port Victoria 24 Dec	87		Port Victoria 16 Feb	Lizard 15 June	119	Cardiff
Winterhude / Holm 3-masted barque	Gothenburg 21 Oct	Port Lincoln 2 Feb	104		Port Germein 22 March	Falmouth 3 August	134	Barrow
Lawhill / Söderlund 4-masted barque	Liverpool 15 Oct	Port Lincoln 8 Jan	85		Port Lincoln 15 March	Falmouth 2 August	140	Glasgow
Killoran / Leman 3-masted barque	Auckland 13 May	Port Lincoln 3 June	21		Port Lincoln 13 July	Queenstown 29 Nov *	139	
Abraham Rydberg / Malmberg 4-masted barque	Rivofjord 24 Aug	Wallaroo 10 Dec	108		Port Germein 18 Feb	Lizard 15 June *	115	Ipswich (120)
Kommodore Johnsen / Peters Clausen 4-masted aux. barque	Auckland 11 Feb	Port Lincoln 2 March	19		Port Lincoln 26 March	Queenstown 11 July	107	Cork

* via Cape of Good Hope

144